Sam's new teacher, Mr Smiley, was OK. H
"OK," he said, one day. "Everyone listen.
school trip."

"We are all going to have a big day out," he said.
"Hurray!" everyone said.
"Where are we going, Mr Smiley?" said Sam.

"We are going to the seaside," said Mr Smiley. "It's a treat! We are going with the Hops Hill Old Folks Club. They will be our guests."

"Oh no!" everyone said.

"Oh yes!" said Mr Smiley. "It will be the best day out ever. You wait and see."

The day of the trip came. Bert's coach pulled up at the school. The old folks were on the coach.

"Quick, get in, kids!" shouted Grandad.

"Oh no!" groaned Sam.

Everyone got on the coach. Mr Smiley stood at the front.
"OK," he said. "Everyone listen! Today you will each look after one of our guests."
"That's one each!" shouted Mrs Cherry.

Ravi and Jo chose to look after Grandad and his mate, Ron. Sam and Kim chose Mrs Cherry and little Betty Drew.

"I don't need looking after," said Mrs Cherry to Sam, "but you'd better keep an eye on that Betty Drew."

"I don't need looking after," said Betty Drew to Kim, "but you'd better keep an eye on that Mrs Cherry."

"Oh no," groaned Sam and Kim.

"Let's have a sing-song!" shouted Ron.

"Yes, a sing-song! A sing-song!" shouted all the old folks.

"Keep right on to the end of the road. Keep right on to the end!" the old folks sang.

"This might be fun after all," said Sam.

Bert stopped the coach at the seaside. They all got out. "OK," said Mr Smiley. "Off you go. We'll meet back here at four o'clock."

"Oo-oo, smell that sea air!" said Mrs Cherry.
"Let's go to the beach, everyone!" shouted Ron.
"To the beach! To the beach!" sang Grandad and Betty Drew.
"To the beach!" sang Kim and Jo.
Off they went!

"Let's get some deckchairs," said Ron.
They all went to get the deckchairs. There was an ice-cream van by the deckchairs.
"Oo-oo, ice-cream!" said Ron and Grandad.
"Ice-creams for everyone!" said Mrs Cherry to the ice-cream man.
"These old folks are OK," said Jo.

Everyone had lots of fun. They dug big holes in the sand.
They splashed in the sea.
"I dare you to go in a boat," said Sam to little Betty Drew.
"I dare," said Betty Drew. "Look at me!"

"Let's play football," said Mrs Cherry. "Old folks against you kids!"
"You're on!" said Sam.
Betty Drew scored a goal!
"Nice one, Betty!" said Mrs Cherry.

After the game, they all sat down.

"Oh no!" said Sam. "Where are Grandad and Ron?"

"I don't know!" said Ravi.

"I bet *I* know where they are," said Mrs Cherry. "Come on!"

They all went down to the sea wall.
There was Grandad. There was Ron. They were holding up a fish.
"Poo! What's that?" said Betty Drew.

"It's a fish! I caught it with my fishing rod!" said Ron.
"He caught it!" said Grandad. "I saw him!"
"Men!" said Mrs Cherry. "Come on, kids."

Kim found a bag for Ron's fish. Then they all sat on the sea wall and had their lunch.

"What shall we do now?" said Ron.

Just then some of the others came along.
"Where are you off to?" said Grandad.
"We're off to the fair," they said.
Betty Drew went pink.
"Oo-oo! I love fairs!" she said.
"Let's go!" said Ron. "Come on!"

All the old folks were at the fair. There were old folks everywhere. Mrs Cherry was heading…

... for a ride on the Whip!

"Everyone on the Whip! I dare you!" she shouted. "Or are you scared?"

"I'm not scared," screamed Kim. "Oo-oo!"

"We're not scared," screamed Ravi and Sam. "Aaaa...!"

"Whee-ee!" screamed Betty Drew. "This is cool!"

When they got off the Whip, it was nearly four o'clock.
"Come on," said Ron. "We're going to be late. Mr Smiley will tell us off! We don't want to be naughty, do we?"
They all ran back to the beach.
"Wait for me!" shouted Betty Drew.

"Well done," said Mr Smiley. "It's four o'clock and everyone is here."
Then they had another treat. The old folks gave everyone fish and chips for tea.
"Fish and chips for everyone!" said Ron.
"Hurray!" everyone cheered.

Full of fish and chips, they set off for home.
"Keep right on to the end of the road!" they sang. "Keep right on to the end!"
They were almost home when... splut! Bang! Crash!
The coach broke down!

"It's the fan belt!" said Bert. "The fan belt has broken!"
"I've got just the thing to mend it with!" said Betty Drew. "You can mend it with my scarf!"
She waved her scarf at Bert.
"Thanks, Betty," said Bert.
"Hurray! Hurray!" everyone cheered.

Everyone cheered again when the coach got back to the school.
"Well, everyone?" said Mr Smiley.
"You were right, Mr Smiley," said Sam. "That was the best day out ever!"